WHITE LIGHT ES

IAN WHITE

FOR FURTHER INFORMATION CONTACT:
AUSTRALIAN BUSH FLOWER ESSENCES
45 BOORALIE ROAD, TERREY HILLS NSW 2084, AUSTRALIA
PHONE: +61 2 9450 1388 FAX: +61 2 9450 2866
EMAIL: info@ausflowers.com.au www.ausflowers.com.au

PUBLISHED BY BUSH BIOTHERAPIES PTY LTD

FIRST PUBLISHED APRIL 2002

ISBN 0-9580590-0-4

TO JANE ROSENSON, AND TO ALL THE STAFF AT AUSTRALIAN BUSH FLOWER ESSENCES, THANK YOU FOR YOUR WONDERFUL HELP AND SUPPORT.

EDITING: JANE ROSENSON AND MANDY SAYER
TEXT DESIGN AND PRODUCTION: RENO DESIGN, SYDNEY R21079
COVER DESIGN: RED RAZOO
PRINTED AND BOUND IN AUSTRALIA BY BPA PRINT GROUP

CONTENTS

PREFACE

THE SPLENDOUR OF MACHU PICCHU, IN THE SACRED VALLEY OF THE INCAS, PERU.

The White Light Essences have been brought through by Spirit to help us invoke and access the realm of Nature and Spirit within ourselves, so as to more fully explore and understand our spirituality and fulfil our highest potential.

This project has taken me over four years to complete and has led me on a journey to some of the most remote and sacred locations around the world. During the past 20 years I have researched and developed the Australian Bush Flower Essences — they have been a stepping stone to bring me to the point in my growth and spirituality where I have been able to make the White Light Essences. They were made with the utmost integrity, humility and love, it is in that spirit that I commend and offer them to you.

In much Love, Light and Respect

IAN WHITE

WATER ESSENCE

IN THE HIGH COUNTRY
ON THE ISOLATED
SOUTHERN END OF THE
ISLE OF IONA, SCOTLAND.

Upon receiving information about the Water Essence I was told to in fact make two remedies and combine them together to make this one Essence. One was to be made from the Northern Hemisphere and the other from the Southern. Also, it was strongly suggested and I would highly recommend that the Water Essence should be the first of the seven White Light Essences to be taken. This chronology allows for the flowing expansion of our reality and consequently paves the way for fully utilising the unique qualities of the other White Light Essences – greatly enhancing and activating them. To do otherwise will appreciably reduce the effectiveness of the results.

The Southern Hemisphere Water Essence was to be prepared on Heron Island on the Great Barrier Reef, one of only a handful of islands off Australia's East Coast, with a reef that you can swim to without needing a boat. If you were to envision an idyllic tropical paradise, then you would end up with an image very close to that of Heron Island. In the clear turquoise water swim many species of turtles, stingrays, sharks and tropical fish, whilst in the winter, migrating pods of whales pass by in all their splendour.

The Water Essence was prepared on top of a large coral head at the waters edge, on the out going tide. As the water gently lapped the sand during its slow withdrawal it created — as it has for thousands of years — a poignant moment for entry into the intense emotion of sadness, which is inherent to the element of water. By the time the Essence preparation was completed, the crowning rim of the coral encasing the bowl was an island in itself, barely rising above and totally surrounded by the water of the incoming tide, 100 metres out from shore.

This remedy integrates the element of Water within you and attunes you to its vibration, and to the Nature Spirit of Water — the Undine. It also allows you to experience intensely any of your own emotional disharmony so that it may then be purified and released. This Essence is appropriate for anyone who isn't choosing to, or feels that they can't, let go of aspects from the past. Not only will it help to release the past but it will also help you from remaining emotionally closed off after a negative or traumatic experience. There may however, be a day or two of strong emotional release — most likely in the form of tears. This release is certainly nothing to be afraid of. This remedy, together with the element of Water, is very nurturing and cleansing, and encourages us all to be more open to receiving.

HERON ISLAND,
GREAT BARRIER REEF,
AUSTRALIA

The Water Essence illuminates the conscious mind so as to reveal and initiate the release of our deepest, most ancient, negative karmic patterns. Another important aspect of this essence is that it can dissolve the boundaries of a person's perceptions and realities.

The location for the other Water Essence was in stark contrast to Heron Island. The small mystical Isle of Iona, only three and a half miles long and one and a half miles across, dotted with only 70 houses, is found off the West Coast of Scotland. Centuries prior to the arrival of St Columba in 563AD, the island had been adopted as a centre of religion by the Druids. St Columba, venerated as one of the greatest of holy men, was largely responsible for the spread of Christianity into England and Scotland. Iona has always been a site of solitude, reflection, spiritual inspiration and initiation, while also being the sacred burial ground of the early Scottish, Irish and Norwegian Kings.

On travelling across to Iona I was met with the shocking news that a hurricane was hitting the area with winds of up to 100 miles an hour along with a forecast of lengthy rain periods that would last many days — hardly the ideal conditions in which to prepare the Essence. Fortunately, with only one day lost due to the rough seas I was able to make it across to Iona, only to be greeted by blue skies and sunny warm weather. The remedy was prepared on the isolated southern end of the island two days later, on the 15th June 2000.

It has often been said that the veil between the spiritual world and the earth is very thin on Iona. Certainly I have found meditating here to be a marvellous experience as it is so easy to both have a sense of and to feel surrounded by the love vibration that is Spirit. In preparing the remedy that day, this feeling was heightened many fold and that very quality was captured in the Essence. The Essence made on Iona shared many qualities of the one from Heron Island – namely that of trusting and nurturing ourselves, being able to find the inner stillness in which to experience our feelings fully and of achieving emotional harmony.

The Essence prepared on Iona creates the deep knowing that whatever challenge one is encountering, you will be all right. It helps one to release the emotional stress and turmoil of a situation so that you can move on and make the necessary choices that will enable you to deal with it, while also assisting you to attain a serene state of inner peace. This remedy is for people who are ready to make

THE PEACEFUL SOLITUDE
AND STUNNING VIEWS OF
IONA, SCOTLAND.

the hard choices in their life. It can totally change the perspective of what direction one will choose. By using this Essence, one will opt for the highest choice — not often the easiest, nor the one that they necessarily want, but rather their choice will invariably be for the highest good of all and for the perfect unfolding of the divine plan.

Heron Island and Iona are both entirely surrounded by the ocean and the sea and the Essences made in these opposite hemispheres provide the polarity necessary to completely experience the Water Essence. In order to achieve this, the unique and shared qualities of these two remedies have been alchemically blended together to become the one Water Essence.

EARTH ESSENCE

THE VILLAGE OF PATAL BHUVANESHWAR, HIGH IN THE HIMALAYAS, INDIA.

On both my two previous trips to India I had been stricken with dysentery, and during the last occasion I nearly died. Thus, it was with a wry smile that I contemplated the message from my inner guidance telling me that I needed to return to the sub-continent once more, to make the Earth Essence. I was told that once there I had to prepare the essence in the cave at Patal Bhuvaneshwar in the north of India. Visiting this cave had been the sole reason why I had gone to India on my last journey.

This region, set high in the Himalayas, is within sight of the Tibetan border and is famous for its striking natural beauty, religious beliefs of its people and temples for which it is called the "Land of Gods". To reach the cave requires three days of extremely difficult driving from the nearest large city, Delhi. The journey proceeds incredibly slowly on crowded, noisy, diesel-stenched roads of the flat plain country. Eventually, these roads lead up into the treacherous, narrow mountainous ones with their dangerous, blind hairpin bends.

To prepare oneself before entering the cave one traditionally must first be blessed and do pujas – Indian rituals and prayers, with the priests at the Shiva Temple of Jageshwar, which is a couple of hours drive from the district capital of Almora. And secondly, bathe nearby in the confluence of the Rameswar and Surayu Rivers in order to spiritually cleanse yourself.

In the ancient Hindu Scriptures there is reference to this cave. According to these texts, the first sighting of this cave temple was obtained by King Rituparna of Ayodhya who became lost whilst hunting. He saw Sheshnag — the mythical cobra and creator of the cave who was standing guard at its opening. Sheshnag lifting the King onto the top of his head took him through the cave, where he observed many of the Hindu Gods including Krishna, Shiva and Ganesh, performing pujas. On leaving the cave the King was forbidden to reveal to anyone what he had seen. Unfortunately, he disobeyed this agreement and instantly died, while the cave was once more hidden from mortal vision. The Scriptures foretold that after being closed for 3,000 years a soldier would rediscover the cave.

In the early 1990s a devotee had a dream where his guru, Sai Baba, took him down into what he believed to be a mystical cave in which there were idols of all the Hindu Gods. This man was a high-ranking officer in the Indian army and in charge of the troops stationed along the Himalayan border with Tibet. Soon after this dream, on a tour of inspection, he came to visit Patal Bhuvaneshwar and was taken to the cave. He immediately realised the cave was the very same one that Sai Baba had shown him in his earlier dream. The officer later had army engineers put in lighting and a generator to help more fully illuminate and reveal the secrets of the cave.

There are many well held beliefs that relate to the cave today. One of the most profound espouses that visiting the cave will clear 21 generations of ancestral karma, while another claims that your full, original, twelve strands of DNA will be restored after entering it! Certainly the first time I went to the cave in 1996 I found it to be a very powerful place. There are 80 rock-hewn stairs leading down from the temple opening deep down through the earth into the main cave. Once down inside, you immediately see a big, naturally occurring rock idol of Sheshnag, the cobra, holding the earth on his hood. From here you walk many metres along the spine of Sheshnag to where water drops from an eight petalled lotus onto the severed head of Ganesh. In Hindu mythology Ganesh's father, Shiva, had beheaded his son but later rejoined his body to the head of an elephant using Sacred Water from an eight-petalled lotus. Throughout the cave complex there are numerous other naturally occurring, carved rock Idols of Hindu Gods and depictions of important images and scenes from the Hindu Scriptures.

One can clearly see a symbolic representation of the River Ganges flowing out of the locks of Lord Shiva. Even the astrological depiction of the Milky Way is quite evident here, as are the four entrance ways which are related to the four eras or epochs on earth. The first door is to that of "Sin", which was closed after the end of the Ravana epoch. The second door symbolises War, which was closed after the Mahabharata era finished. The third entrance, of Dharma, is to be closed at the end of this current era, Kaliyug. The fourth entrance leads to Moksha (enlightenment) which will be closed after the end of the next era to follow — Satyug. There is also within the cave complex a set of four lingas representing these four eras and predicts when our current era will end.

I had timed this essence-making trip to coincide with the full moon, though I was rather nervous about whether the head priest Shree Bhandari would grant me permission to make the Essence in the cave — one is not allowed to enter unless accompanied by a priest. On the actual day of the full moon, permission was obtained but unfortunately the man who operated the generator and who had the key to it could not be found at the appointed hour. After a frustrating and fruitless search by myself, the head priest and other villagers for this fellow, I reluctantly accepted that the Essence would have to be made the following day.

INSIDE THE CAVE AT PATAL BHUVANESHWAR DEPICTING THE EIGHT PETALLED LOTUS (TOP CENTRE) DRIPPING WATER TO WHERE GANESH WAS BEHEADED BY HIS FATHER, SHIVA.

That night I was drawn to do an earth healing in a smaller, completely different cave further along from the main entrance. It was there under a starlit Himalayan night that I had the understanding that it was more appropriate to be making the Essence the next day on the waning moon as during this phase of the lunar cycle there is more energy going back into the earth — it was an Earth Essence after all! I was told not only would this Essence be for grounding but also to teach patience!

Other spiritual aspects of this Essence include being able to tune into the subtle realms and vibrations. The Essence also fosters a strong connection, respect and reverence to nature, the Ancients, the earth nature spirits, the earth, the life force, life and the origins of life. The Earth Essence also helps to heal internal structure and order in life and is a very important grounding remedy, especially for those doing a lot of spiritual work. Quite importantly, this remedy enables light workers to find their drive and to move forward with purpose. In the spiritual field there are many people moving forward but in a scattered way. They are putting in a lot of effort but getting nowhere fast. This Essence will allow them to be centred, grounded and to find their direction and then to proceed forward with clarity and focus. It also creates a wonderful sense of deep restfulness especially in the heart and base chakras.

The following day at Bhuvanshwar, everything proceeded smoothly including permission being given for me to take down all the necessary equipment such as bowls, decanters, brandy and water that I would need to make the remedy. I am not sure whether the head priest fully understood what I was attempting to do down in the cave, however, he was a very wise man and must have known on some level the importance of what was to be created. I also felt that he perceived my respect for this sacred site and the integrity of my intentions. As well, he did remember me from my last trip and knew I had journeyed far to get here on each occasion. Once down in the cave he very graciously allowed me private space to both tune into the vibrational energy there and to prepare the remedy. Thankfully, he let me leave the bowl, filled with the Essence, in the cave overnight, so as to fully absorb the vibration of the cave which was necessary to complete the remedy. Normally no one is allowed to take photos inside the cave complex, but the next morning this too was generously offered to me, much to my surprise.

By initially taking the Water Essence, you can then activate the other Essences more deeply. The Water Essence, by helping to dissolve away the limitations of where you believe you are capable of going, prepares the way for the Earth Essence to then take you beyond your old reference points and limitations.

Another very important quality of the Earth Essence is that it helps establish a connection with the Manu of a country. The Manu, which are part of the Spiritual Hierarchy could be likened to being the Higher Self of a particular country, and has dominion over all the Nature Spirits and Devas of that land. By establishing a connection with the Manu you can access the essence or vibrational quality of that country which is very useful if, for example, you were to be doing spiritual work there but unable to be physically present. By helping you to energetically access that country, the Earth Essence, allows you to be more effective in your work. In such a way, the Earth Essence helps open the doorway to wherever you want to direct your spiritual work on the planet — with or without a visa!

On an emotional level this essence helps to bring stability to relationships and people having problems in committing to one. The latter could be either as a result of past trauma or of never having had a role model where commitment was evident. A person who is in a relationship only because being with that partner is better than any other option at the moment may decide to end such a relationship after taking the Earth Essence — as they will realise at some level, that their deeper needs are not being met. This allows the space for another person to enter one's life, a person with whom one will feel compelled to create a committed relationship.

Travelling in India is a rich and stimulating experience, though also incredibly intense and challenging and I was very relieved to be able to leave this time with not only the Earth Essence but also with my health more or less intact. However, the thought of having to both frequently return to India as well as climbing the Putacusi mountain in Peru to replenish the mother tinctures of the Earth and Angelic Essences is somewhat daunting. Ah, the joys of essence-making!

FIRE ESSENCE

THE LANDSCAPE
ANGEL OF KATAJUTA,
CENTRAL AUSTRALIA.

The Fire Essence was made amongst the magnificent red rock domes in the sacred area known as either Katajuta, the Aboriginal name, or The Olgas, which represents both the physical and spiritual centre of Australia. I was extremely happy to receive the message that I needed to return to my beloved Olgas to make the Fire Essence, as I hardly need any excuse to go back to this remarkable area. I have been visiting this region annually for the last 15 years and find it an incredibly renewing place for my spirit.

The energy here is exceptionally powerful. Traditionally, Katajuta is a wandering place for men. I love going there, especially in the dark of the early morning before the sun rises, when I can literally have the place all to myself. In fact I can frequently spend the entire day wandering about Katajuta in blissful solitude without seeing anyone — well, not anyone in a physical form anyway.

On this particular day in late Autumn I set out long before the sunrise, as the location I wanted in the South-East of Katajuta required four hours of walking to reach, but once there it offered superb majestic views of the early morning sun over Uluru.

In the preceding few months the entire Centre of Australia had been inundated with prolonged heavy rains, the likes of which had not been seen for over 30 years. The effect was unbelievable. The arid stony desert of the inland, known as the Red Centre, had become green and alive with carpets of intensely coloured flowers of all hues, especially the reds and purples. Tens of thousands of birds had also migrated to take advantage of the myriad of insects and the seemingly overnight populations of frogs and fish created in the waters of the previously dry inland lakes and rivers.

I had never seen the Centre looking like this. It was the perfect environment to make the Essence. Not only did the remedy take on the ancient healing qualities of the Olgas but it also encompassed the passion, creation, possibilities and potential of Fire. One aspect of the four Elemental White Light Essences — Fire, Water, Air and Earth — is that they help you to connect, embody and master that element while also aligning you to the Nature Spirit of each particular Element. The Fire Nature Spirit, or Elemental Being — the Salamander — is always associated with and ever present alongside the bees and butterflies. At the moment of completion of the Fire Essence, under the hot sun on top of one of the domes of Katajuta, I looked up to find myself surrounded by butterflies. The magical synchronicity of this moment was a wonderful confirmation and crowning of this alchemic experience.

On this day the red rock domes with their vulva and womb-like cave formations, seemed to be glowing like molten fire. Their shapes and formations strongly suggested sensuality, passion, sexuality and creation — all aspects of fire.

THE EXACT LOCATION IN KATAJUTA WHERE THE FIRE ESSENCE WAS PREPARED. ON THE LEFT OF THE HORIZON ULURU (AYERS ROCK) CAN BE SEEN.

Traditionally Fire has been associated with the burning off of one's dross — or impurities, especially that of the astral body. The higher astral plane, which addresses the elevation of consciousness, is directly linked to the same intense colour as that of fire, namely orange.

The Fire Essence has a strong connection with a primordial time at the very beginning of intelligence on earth. This Essence can open people to their most ancient source; back to the moment when the soul originally chose the life purpose for its earthly incarnations. This remedy helps to unlock the most sacred part of an individual, revealing one of the last bastions of inner secrets and ancient knowledge that a person possesses — their original and on-going life paths. When this is revealed an individual will be left with a "fiery" sense of purpose and direction. Consequently, he or she is inspired and motivated to follow their life path and fulfil their highest destiny. There is no middle ground with this essence. There is no where to go except forward. Before working with this Essence an individual will have to be clear if he or she wants irreversible change. One must, deep in their heart or soul, be prepared to move forward no matter what the consequences. It is only then that this Essence will work. The Fire Essence reveals the big picture and I assure you it will be a compelling one.

For the full potency of this Essence to be realised, there are two other necessary components that need to be incorporated with the use of this remedy. First of all, it should be taken only after initially working with the Water Essence. The latter will pave the way and allow an individual to then experience the deepest action of the Fire Essence. Secondly, it is important to find the right sound vibration to work with that will resonate with the person who is going to take this remedy. Sound, is the force inherent in all things and has a very powerful effect on the cellular structure of human beings. It can harmonise dissonant frequencies both in and around us. Sound, through its vibrationary pattern, helps structure the patterns of order in Nature and has a profound effect on our psyche. We can trace this concept back to our most important spiritual texts. The Hindu's, in their Veddas say,

"IN THE BEGINNING WAS BRAHMAN WITH WHOM WAS THE WORD. AND THE WORD IS BRAHMAN."

Whilst in the Christian bible we have,

"IN THE BEGINNING WAS THE WORD, AND WORD WAS WITH GOD, AND THE WORD WAS GOD...AND THE WORD WAS MADE FLESH."

Many years ago I was taught an ancient system of numerology by Glynn Braddy that revealed each individual's master number, which in turn corresponded with a specific colour. Associated with each colour was a musical composition that would help balance any individual whose master number corresponded to that particular colour. It is my understanding that sound – along with the use of the Water and Fire Essences – is also necessary to unlock that sacred part

THE SITE (TOP RIGHT) WHERE THE FIRE ESSENCE WAS PREPARED IN KATAJUTA.

within yourself. For each individual, their specific sound vibration is highly likely to be the piece of music corresponding to their colour.

My wife, harpist Jane Rosenson, and violinist Kirsten Williams, both exceptional musicians, have recorded a CD with excerpts from all of the musical compositions pertaining to this system of numerology. So, simply by listening daily to this CD during the time you are taking the two remedies, you will be provided with the musical key to access the ancient knowledge within you of your life path. Well over 90 percent of people will find their appropriate sound vibration on this CD. Alternatively there may be another piece of music or sound that you intuitively know will be the right one for you to work with.

A very interesting aspect of this Essence is that it will either work brilliantly, if you are totally in-tune and ready to take a major step forward in your life, or it won't work at all. Again, there is no middle ground to this Essence!

AIR ESSENCE

THE LAKE OF ST WOLFGANG
WITH THE AUSTRIAN ALPS
IN THE BACKROUND, FROM
THE TOP OF SCHAFBERG
MOUNTAIN, AUSTRIA.

This essence was made over the 9th and 10th June 1999 on top of Schafberg Mountain, St Wolfgang, Austria. I happened by chance to discover the Wolfgangsee and surrounding lakes after trusting a gut feeling one day whilst driving between Vienna and Salzburg and headed off the main autobahn. All the lakes in this region, known locally as Salzkammergut, are incredibly beautiful, but to me St Wolfgang is even more exquisite. There is a pervasive purity and serenity to be found there, while nestled behind St Wolfgang is the imposing Schafberg Mountain. The latter is especially famous for its vista, which is quite unrivalled in magnificence. From its summit 14 lakes are visible. It is located right in the heart of the Austrian Alps, surrounded by snow capped peaks with a view that extends across the plain beyond the Danube as far as Southern Bohemia. As one early explorer exclaimed, as he stood on the top of this powerful mountain:

"A HEART UNMOVED BY SO MUCH BEAUTY IS SURELY
TO BE PITIED AS IT CANNOT KNOW NATURE'S GREAT BOOK,
NOR PENETRATE THE MARVELS CONCEALED IN IT."

The appeal of this spot had drawn me a number of times prior to making the Essence there. As is Spirit's want, they once more directed me to go to the most difficult and dangerous location to make a remedy! All I can think is that they must take great delight in seeing me crawl precariously on all fours along narrow, knife-edged, rocky precipices of great height, loaded up to the gun-whales with bottles of brandy, water, bowls and other paraphernalia. However, Spirit did at least keep people away from the area whilst I was tuning in and preparing the Essence.

With all the White Light Essences and indeed any of my Australian Bush Flower Essences, I have been told that it is critical not to have the thought forms of any other person present while the remedy is being made. Even people wandering by and looking on, innocent as that may seem, is enough to contaminate the vibration of the remedy being created. When making these Essences it requires a great deal of time and focus to both physically and psychically prepare the exact location where the bowl is to be placed, and to protect it. I then invoke and bring down the wisdom of the Ancients and the Elements, to hold and maintain the energy while also attuning to and co-operating with the Landscape Angel of the area, the Nature Spirits and Devas. During these times I am inevitably surrounded by a multitude of beings from the Brotherhood of Light.

Normally I stay next to the bowl during the entire duration of making the remedy, which can last between one and a half and two and a half hours. However, after the Air Essence had already been left 'brewing' in the sun for two hours, I was instructed to let the bowl remain out overnight on the mountain and to decant the remedy the following morning. This would allow the Air Essence to go through the blackness of the night, enabling it to embody the divine guidance and protection that accompanies one when they too go through the darkness. I could have stayed out with the bowl as well, however, I probably would have frozen to death! That night a glowing, golden orange full moon rose over the Alps. Dawn was heralded with a layered sky of intense pink and mauve hues. As the remedy was decanted a flock of birds, which is closely connected to the Nature Spirit of Air – the Sylph, descended and circled over me as I completed the final stages of the Essence preparation.

During my attunement prior to making the remedy, I was informed that the Air Essence (What other Essence could it be when made at such a height?) had the quality of allowing a person to journey out to much further realms and levels on the Spiritual plane. This quality is clearly evident as a doctrine of signature of the remedy when you contemplate the vast expansive vista from Schafberg Mountain. I experienced an extremely blissful state of love and heart opening to both the divine and to nature throughout the duration of preparing the Essence. It was an unbelievably sweet and tender time.

The Essence itself produces a sensation of feeling light, easy and carefree. The message that came from the remedy to a colleague of mine Peter Tadd, an exceptional American intuitive working in Ireland, was that it would assist one's thought processes to become more flowing and gentle. It isn't our moods that always change but rather our thoughts — and they can be easy and flowing, or not. If it were the latter, then this Essence would be of great benefit.

During my time meditating with this Essence I was flooded with insights concerning its healing qualities. I was told that when making a choice, the Air Essence helps one to maintain a balance between an intellectual and an emotional approach, whilst also aiding discrimination and discernment. Whenever you are needing to make a decision within an emotionally charged situation, the Air Essence will enable you to feel stable, more in control and empowered. Consequently it is an excellent remedy for people going through

THE NARROW, KNIFE-EDGED ROCKY PRECIPICE OF SCHAFBERG MOUNTAIN, WHERE THE AIR ESSENCE WAS PREPARED.

emotional stress and trauma. I sensed that this remedy, made literally on the top of the world, would help you to see the overview of any problem and not get caught up in the detail or the drama of it. At the same time it enhances your guidance and inner knowing in order to deal with the situation more effectively. The Essence simultaneously promotes the realisation that life will go on and meanwhile to simply feel the love and the peace around you; to know and to trust that you are forever protected and guided by God and his instruments in the spiritual realm, whilst here on earth. Always remember that this Essence can invoke peace and harmony and to let it reign within your heart and mind. It helps you to see life as being simple and to keep it simple, surrendering to God any problem, no matter what the circumstances, knowing that there is always love and peace overlighting everything — feel this and know it!

ANOTHER ANGLE OF THE SITE WHERE THE AIR ESSENCE WAS PREPARED, AT SUNRISE.

The Air Essence has the potential to bring out a person's spirituality to the highest degree with integrity and passion, while at the same time allowing one to bend and alter his or her reality in a very profound way. My friend Kachina, a gifted Australian psychic and light worker who has provided me with many insights regarding these Essences, proclaimed this remedy "The Mary Poppins Essence". In the movie of the same name, this character is practically perfect in every way; she is firm, she is strong, yet at the same time operates with insight and integrity; she has no limitations, expectations or attachments. She is totally at one with everything. This Essence brings out one's "Mary Poppins" qualities: that ability to perform miracles as if they were a commonplace occurrence, but at the same time appreciating the ordinariness of everyday life.

The remedy enables people to understand that they are indeed a miracle and all their actions are miraculous. Yet it hinders one from becoming conceited from this knowledge, rather allowing them to remain humble and lighthearted. The Air Essence honours, acknowledges and reflects to us our uniqueness, holiness, sacredness, and perfection.

HIGHER SELF ESSENCE

PALENQUE RUINS, MEXICO

Higher Self was the first of The White Light Essences, which was made on the 25th March 1999 at Palenque, Mexico. However, the origin of this Essence began at Palenque in the January of the previous year when I first came to this amazing place. I had heard about these ancient Incan ruins sometime before and had been very keen to visit, but I was unprepared for the intense reaction that I had there. It was very much a "homecoming place" for me. The tranquillity there, coupled with the majestic spirituality of the ruins and the vibrancy of the surrounding countryside, made Palenque a truly remarkable experience. Grace, my daughter, who at the time was nine-years-old and accompanying me on the trip, was continually rolling her eyes on that first morning, in response to my gushing enthusiasm on entering Palenque. I kept exclaiming,

"ISN'T THIS FANTASTIC! ISN'T IT WONDERFUL HERE!
CAN YOU FEEL THE ENERGY?"

After many hours spent wandering through the site I came upon a small temple on the edge of the ruins. Upon entering I felt a strong sense to quietly sit and meditate there. It was a very deep and powerful meditation, though at the end of it I received a message that disturbed me a great deal. I was told to leave the rose quartz crystal that I was carrying with me there in the temple. This, however, was not any common run of the mill crystal. I had had it with me for over two years, starting from a trip to India where I'd taken it to the Ganges, the Cave at Bhubaneswar and the Sai Baba Ashram. Two years prior to this Indian trip, I had been shown a vision of Grace on her wedding day.

It was an incredibly moving and heartfelt experience. I was left feeling so elated and indescribably happy after I saw her joy and radiance on that day and was then overtaken with tears and tremendous pride, realising what a beautiful person she had grown up to become. Consequently I had decided to take this particular rose quartz crystal with me to India and all future travels, to sacred or high energy centres on the planet. My intention was to present this vibrationally charged crystal to my daughter on her wedding day. However, here in the temple, in the exquisite atmosphere of Palenque, I was being told to bury the crystal and leave it behind. Initially, I struggled with this but eventually decided to listen to my Higher Self and to the instructions I was receiving. After burying the crystal I was left with a strong sense of sadness.

THE TEMPLE IN PALENQUE WHERE BOTH THE CRYSTAL WAS BURIED AND THE HIGHER SELF ESSENCE WAS PREPARED.

The next day I returned to the ruins and this time in my meditation I was told that I would be returning to Palenque sometime in the future to prepare an Essence. The message continued that it would not be a Flower Essence but rather an Essence of Palenque itself. Furthermore, the rose quartz crystal that I had buried there was to be dug up and used as the crucial element in the making of the Essence. The importance of leaving the rose quartz in the ground was for it to act as a conduit to absorb the energy and vibration of Palenque. It was with great trepidation that I re-entered Palenque 14 months later. Would my crystal still be there? Would I be able to find it? What if it was not there, and what shape and form would this new Essence take? In the past I had only worked with flowers in making an essence and I wandered if I would be able to effectively capture the energy of Palenque in a remedy.

I had previously concealed the crystal very carefully under a pillar in the old temple. I slid my hand into the earth in the base of the pillar and began to panic when I could not find it. But a loud message kept going through my head — It is okay, it is there, trust. When I relaxed, my fingers brushed against something smooth — it was the crystal! For the next two days I was happy to merely walk around Palenque, meditating and soaking up the unique vibrations there, waiting for the right time to make the remedy. On the morning of the third day, I had a strong sense that the moment had arrived.

Whilst tuning in to make the remedy I was told that this would be the first of a small select range of Essences to be made by me at sacred sites, scattered throughout the world, that would greatly enhance many aspects of one's spirituality. Another important message that I received at this time was that the Essence I was about to make here was not so much a Palenque Essence but rather, was to be the Higher Self Essence.

The very pure, refined and crystal clear vibration of Palenque, a remnant from the ancient Incan era, allows one to align to and access their Higher Self. The Essence prepared there encapsulates these very same qualities. My own personal test the previous year in Palenque had been a vital component necessary to birth this Essence. For without following the directive from my Higher Self and giving up my personal attachment to the rose quartz crystal, this Essence would never have come about.

The Higher Self Essence funnels and channels energy of the highest order into one's very core, from where it will radiate out and expand dramatically. Those who are balanced in their Spirituality will have the possibility to be totally expanded. This Essence helps us to be aware of what is beyond the physical experience and can help one tap into sources of ancient wisdom and knowledge.

Our Higher Self is comprised of every lifetime we have ever had and this Essence offers the opportunity to help a person connect with these earlier incarnations.

LUSH CANOPIES OF TREES ARE ALWAYS THREATENING TO HIDE THE RUINS AND MYSTERY OF PALENQUE ONCE MORE. THE TEMPLE CAN BE SEEN ON THE FAR RIGHT.

After taking this remedy the most likely time you will tap into these past lives will either be in the dream state, in meditation, or simply when you're day dreaming. You will then be able to beam back the energy of whatever it is that you are needing from that past time. It would be advisable to take this remedy when you are feeling very grounded and balanced. If you don't you may have trouble being anchored in present time, as you may be shifting between the past and present extremely quickly. Kachina received a message that the Higher Self Essence can also open dimensional doorways and allow one to enter/access alternate realities. Thus further highlighting the powerful potential of this Essence.

DEVIC ESSENCE

WATER FROM THE RED OR BLOOD SPRING IS PIPED FROM THE CHALICE WELL DOWN THE GARDEN TO EMERGE AT THE LION'S HEAD.

This Essence was prepared on the summer solstice on the 21st June 2000 in the Chalice Well Garden in Glastonbury, England, an amazing sanctuary of beauty, serenity and peacefulness. Many spiritual workers claim that there is a major leyline making a triangular link between three of the highest energy centres in the United Kingdom — Iona, Findhorn and Glastonbury.

The Well itself can be traced back to early Roman times shortly after the crucifixion of Christ, whilst the water flowing from it has been revered for its purity and healing power as far back as the 16th century. The well is fed by a spring of primary water, Chalybeate in nature — or rich in iron, which stains the various water channels red and hence accounts for it being known as the Blood Spring. A smaller spring known as the White Spring also flows through the garden and later joins the Red Spring.

Glastonbury, the home of Arthurian legends and the original setting for the mystical Avalon, is today still vibrantly rich in Celtic tradition and folklore. For many, the red and white springs symbolize the blood and sweat of Christ. It has been the long held belief for many centuries that the Holy Grail, which held the blood and sweat of Christ, is buried in the nearby Glastonbury Tor.

The Chalice Well Gardens have always been a sacred site attracting pilgrims from all around the world, especially in the second half of the last century. In 1967 Wellesley Tudor Pole recreated the setting of the room in Jerusalem where Jesus hosted the Last Supper in the loft in one of the three old houses on the property; based on Pole's far memory vision of it. Ever since it has always been a room set aside for the singular purpose of silent reflection and meditation. I did a prolonged meditation in this very same room the night before making the Essence, hoping to obtain the understanding as to what this Essence would address. Surprisingly, I received nothing at all. However, upon leaving the room and entering the moonlit garden where I recommenced my meditation, the awareness and understanding I was seeking of how this Essence would work was immediately given to me. The irony of having to be outdoors, amongst the Devas, to appreciate how the Devic Essence would work was not lost on me and made me laugh quietly to myself. Every plant, shrub or tree has its own Deva; in fact, so does every manufactured item. Though the Devas — which could be likened to the Guardian Angel that each human has, assigned to plants and nature are generally of a higher vibration.

Early the next morning I began preparing the Essence in a far corner of the garden surrounded by white (symbolic of purity and spirituality) flowers with golden (spiritual wisdom) stamens and masses of dark green (inner peace and harmony) leaves. For me an important aspect of my Essence preparing ritual is to reciprocate with a gift, in heartfelt gratitude, back to the area from where I make an Essence and to the Beings of Light and the Nature Spirits who have helped me in my work there. When the Devic Essence was

GLASTONBURY TOR SEEN THROUGH THE SPLENDID CHALICE WELL GARDEN, GLASTONBURY, UK.

THE WELL LID THAT COVER
THE SHAFT LEADING
9 FEET DOWN TO THE ANCIENT
CHALICE WELL BELOW.

completed I reached into my pocket for the offering I was going to leave — a green serpentine rock I had collected in Iona a few days earlier when making the Water Essence. However my hand felt nothing, the rock was not there. I realised that I must have left it in my room by mistake. But then I quickly received the message that I had already left a gift a year earlier! On that occasion I had started to prepare the very same Essence but in an enclosed section of the Chalice Well Garden known as Arthur's Court. However it had been necessary to abandon the project halfway through because the gardener had entered the area to empty its small healing pool, thereby vibrationally contaminating the remedy.

I've always adhered to the message I'd received telling me that it is crucial for both the White Light Essences and my Australian Bush Flower Essences that no other person's thought forms be present while I am making these remedies. Beforehand I had placed a few of my crystals under the small waterfall that cascades down into Arthur's court so as to cleanse and purify them. But when I returned to collect them a few hours later one of them was missing. I searched everywhere for it without luck. It was a complete mystery to me how it could have vanished. That particular crystal, a danburite, is used for communication with the Devas! So, that was my gift, given a year in advance. This Devic Essence made on the solstice helps to establish very strong links with the Devic kingdom, while its spiritual healing quality returns one to a place of simplicity and blissful peace. It brings about a feeling of total oneness – being at one with absolutely everything and far less concerned and preoccupied with the hassle and problems of life.

The Holy Grail is closely intertwined with the question of destiny and with Glastonbury. The Devic Essence made from here also addresses this theme. It will help you to remember why you are here, and assist those who remember their destiny to take action and become more passionate about their life path once again — provided that they are tuned in. If not, or if they don't have any drive or motivation, then they are not going to receive the benefit of this quality from the Essence. It is important to be on the right track, but you can still get run over by that train if you ever stop or lose your momentum!

The Devic Essence assists us to care for ourselves on a spiritual level and brings about a devotional, nurturing quality within us for ourselves and others as well as nature. It helps us to understand and to judiciously exercise stewardship, responsibility, protection, caring and loving in our life. Following on from this theme Peter Tadd received this message of the Essence after tuning into it,

"I AM THE INTELLIGENCE BEYOND INTELLIGENCE,
THE ORIGIN OF INTELLIGENCE IN CONSCIOUSNESS."

Peter went on to add that he perceives that Consciousness is the ability to be aware and compassionate of our circumstances; to be truthful and to be aligned with the Over-lighting Beings that govern the evolutionary cycle of the species, of every organism. The taking of the Devic Essence releases within ones auric field a purplish pink and orange band of colour that has an uplifting effect on our psyche. It enables one to contact and communicate with nature, and to listen to any message the plant kingdom has for us. This remedy attunes you with qualities such as healing, from the Devic kingdom. Whenever a person is ungrounded or out of control then this remedy will help to earth them – connecting them back to nature. The Devic Essence is very good to soothe and calm those who are stressed out, wound up, stuck for time or feel disconnected. It is my belief that this remedy will also be useful for anyone who is obsessive or insecure in relationships as often these people carry too many expectations and the essence will help them to feel safe and secure.

The Devic Essence allows us to appreciate the great importance of knowing and remembering that we are a soul being that has, but is not, a physical body. Consequently, the remedy can be also considered for people close to passing over, helping them to attain acceptance and to be clear in the understanding that there is much more beyond our limited reality.

ANGELIC ESSENCE

IN THE REALM OF THE
ANGELS, HIGH ABOVE,
ON THE TOP OF PUTUCUSI,
THE ANDES, PERU.

This Essence was made in Peru on the 28th March 2000 on the top of Putucusi, one of the most sacred mountains to the ancient Incas. To the Incas, Putucusi was an important pivotal point or axis in the world. They used this solitary mountain as a sight for an astronomical centre because it permitted unobstructed observation of both the sunrise and sunset all year round, and a wonderful celestial canopy at night — ideal for their study of the stars. Two concentric circles of soaring forest-covered mountains surround Putucusi, which rises out of the Sacred Valley of the Incas. The first circle of mountains enclosing Putucusi includes Machu Picchu, the spectacular orchid draped, mysterious, remote ruin perched on a crag above a mighty and precipitous gorge of the Urubamba River.

After a number of days exploring these incredible ruins and various trails, I became increasingly curious as to where I would be directed to make the Angelic Essence. Each day on leaving Aguas Calientes, the nearest town to Machu Picchu, to make the journey up to the ruins; I would be filled with awe — not only of the architectural splendour and power of suggestion at this site, but also by the sheer vertical rise of Putucusi. On my third day there I started to get a niggling feeling that maybe Spirit would want me to make the remedy on top of Putucusi. I tried to ignore this intuition but I should have known that Spirit would definitely choose the hardest and most difficult place to make the Essence!

The next day I set out to climb Putucusi but it was not very clear to me where the trail actually started and a couple of hours were lost until I commenced the ascent. What followed were some of the most dangerous moments of my life. I can't remember ever feeling as much fear as I did on that day as I looked up

MACHU PICCHU, THE AWE INSPIRING SIGHT THAT AWAITS ONE AT THE END OF THE INCA TRAIL.

and realised that the climb would involve going straight up to the cloud obscured peak way above, on long sections of totally vertical, old, slippery and mossy wooden rungs — some of which I later found had rotted! The Incas called these the "Stairs of the Sky". My Peruvian guide, a veteran of the Inca Trail that I had been travelling with for the previous few weeks, who was very adroit at rock hopping along these high, narrow and precarious mountain tracks, refused to go up with me, saying that, 'it was too scary even for him!' To make matters worse I was over laden with bowls, brandy, water and photographic equipment necessary for making the Essence — all strapped to my back. The weight and sheer bulk of my load nearly made me fall backwards off the ladder a number of times.

Before starting down at the bottom I honestly thought that I could be killed trying to climb this mountain as I realised that with one slip I would hurtle to my death. Ah, the joy of essence-making! To ease my fear I focused solely on each single step, one at a time, never daring to look neither up nor down, and I took frequent doses of Emergency Essence! By the time I made it to the top I was unable to tell if I was dripping wet from constant rain that fell during the climb or from sweat as a result of all the fear that I had experienced in getting there.

However, the view from the top was truly spectacular and I felt justly rewarded. Looking down on the ruins of Machu Picchu from this great height it was evident that the city had been designed in the shape of the powerful Being, the Cayman, who looks similar to a giant crocodile. Also discernible was how the beautifully made stone complex had been constructed in the image of a majestic condor flying toward the west – towards the Milky Way. In the rich Andean oral tradition there is a legend about a mythical bird known as Llulli. It is told that whenever mankind descends into a state of disorder and decay, the Sun sends down his messenger Llulli – a huge bird of striking vibrant plumage, similar to, though even bigger than, the worlds largest bird, the condor. Llulli's presence in the sky creates a mysterious influence and an atmosphere of love that reduces the human desire to fight or wage war. While soaring over the Sacred Valley of the Incas, Llulli would leave behind a trail of light as he flew towards the west, to the meeting with the night when the Milky Way appears and mankind is transported with the Llulli to the truth, going beyond time, to the idea of God.

Whenever the ancient Incas found a remarkable and stunning natural wonder they attempted to pay homage there and worship God by creating a magnificent structure. Here in Machu Picchu the work of man and nature blend together in a stunning crucible. This site, hidden on a crest of the mountain, is recognised not only as one of the great mysteries of the world but one of the most precious legacies of humanity.

On the top of Putucusi it felt as if I were high above the clouds, in the heavens — the perfect place to make the Angelic Essence. The Incas believed that the Apu — their name for the Angels, who guided and protected men, resided high up in the mountain peaks. Time stood still for me whilst meditating there and I felt I was transported to a realm of incredible clarity and perception. Upon opening my eyes I was greeted by a huge double rainbow spanning the cloud shrouded peaks in front of me. The understanding of this Essence that I was given in my meditation was to purify the aspirations of people to their utmost potential, beyond that of simply a physical or material nature, to raise them to the highest realm — to the Spiritual. Right up until the moment of our death, the Angels are always attempting to inspire and raise our awareness to the spiritual — so that we will look up and embrace the Light. For if we succeed in doing so then there is a purification that flows down to us which can wash away some of our denser material dross. This Essence helps us to be more open to receiving from on high, the Angelic tones of inspiration, love, awareness, communication, guidance and instruction which can lead us to an infinite range of potential possibilities in our mortal lives. The Angelic Essence brings the energy from heaven directly down to earth, uniting the two.

The Angels help us in all our activities, especially in work and service. This Essence enables one to aspire beyond the physical while keeping us connected to the mundane as well. It helps us realise that the spiritual exists in everything and to transcend the deceptive illusion of the physical. The Angelic Essence allows one to have closer contact with the Angelic realm. One can also invoke protection of an Angelic kind and of any specific Angel by taking this Essence.

Another aspect of the Angelic Essence is that it helps to connect you to and access all of the Earth's leylines and energy points. When the earth's grid systems and leylines were first established they contained the potential to project a holographic grid system into the future with all the knowledge and wisdom that humanity would need to take its next big steps. If you have this knowledge and are sufficiently attuned, then you can access these energy points and obtain that information and understanding. You also need to have the highest integrity and

THE MAJESTIC, IMPOSING PUTUCUSI RISING POWERFULLY FROM THE FLOOR OF THE SACRED VALLEY OF THE INCAS. THE ANGELIC ESSENCE WAS PREPARED ON THE VERY PEAK OF THIS MOUNTAIN.

posess true humility to access these points. The Angelic Essence provides not only a key to ancient knowledge but also to future wisdom. On the emotional level this essence is for people with selective hearing, where there are many things they don't particularly want to hear – or see! This remedy removes the blockages which will result in them having to 'see and hear' everything, whether they like it or not! The Angelic Essence also produces a sense of empowerment, especially in relationships and stressful situations by creating mental clarity. The remedy can alleviate and clear our past patterns and blockages, allowing us to respond in a more appropriate way rather than merely reacting.

My hand was nearly cramping as I attempted to scribble down on paper as quickly as I could all the insights and messages from the meditation, anxious not to lose one skerrick of it. Nor did I want to miss this unique opportunity to capture on film the rainbow over the mist-framed mountains. That afternoon on the top of Putucusi there was an amazing vista from every angle. It was only the using up of all my rolls of film that stopped me photographing for longer. However, by now the light was starting to fade and I knew I would be faced with the daunting task of descending most of the journey down in the dark.

The last glimmer of light totally faded about half way down — at least I couldn't tell how far it was to the bottom then! When I arrived at the base of the final set of ladders I knew ahead of me lay a long narrow trail through the rainforest to the road. In daylight it had taken nearly an hour to trek. Much of this final leg was completed slowly on all fours as I tried to make sure in that pitch blackness that I was always staying on the track. At least three or four times I had completely no idea where the track was or which way to go next, and on each of these occasions, in that moment, fire flies appeared, glowing with just enough light for me to make out where the path was. After an arduous couple of hours of crawling, I could see the bright beam of a torch. Cautiously calling out to it, I was greeted by the very concerned and friendly voice of my Peruvian guide. Was I ever so happy and relieved. He had earlier seen me on top of Putucusi but when I had not returned to the inn that evening he had become worried and set out to see if he could find me. He was very glad to have discovered me after I had already reached the bottom of the "Stairs of the Sky", as he certainly would have been in a great dilemma with the prospect of having to climb those treacherous rungs in the darkness.

When I finally got into the town I was dishevelled, starving and totally exhausted but also feeling almost delirious with delight and satisfaction at having successfully completed such a dangerous essence-making adventure — and living to tell the tale.

ADMINISTERING THE ESSENCES

THE LAKE OF ST WOLFGANG
FROM THE TOP OF SCHAFBERG
MOUNTAIN, AUSTRIA.

The White Light Essences work best when taken individually one Essence at a time. The Essences should be taken for two weeks and at the end of that period you can either repeat this Essence or commence another one. It is highly recommended that the first one to be taken is the Water Essence.

PREPARATION

Dosage bottles are prepared by taking a 15ml (or 1/2 oz.) dropper bottle filled with three quarters purified water and one quarter brandy as a preservative and adding seven drops from the stock bottle.

After the stock has been added, the dosage bottle can be lightly shaken or tapped to release its energy. Some people also energise their Essences with a prayer or invocation, or with a visualisation such as surrounding the Essence with white or gold light, though none of these is essential.

DOSAGE

Seven (7) drops of the dosage bottle are taken, under the tongue, on rising and retiring usually for a two week period.

WHITE LIGHT ESSENCES RANGE

The White Light Essences have been brought through by Spirit to help us invoke and access the realm of Nature and Spirit within ourselves, so as to more fully explore and understand our spirituality and fulfil our highest potential.

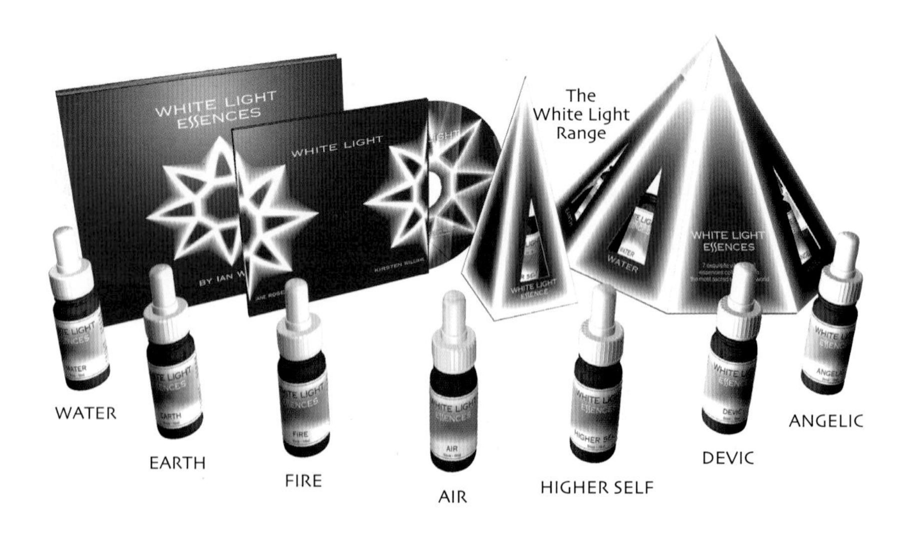

White Light Essence Pyramid Pack

The White Light Essence pyramid pack has been carefully developed to embrace and protect the beauty and potency of these wonderful essences. The White Light Essence pyramid pack contains all 7 spiritual stock essences, Ian's new book and the White Light CD.

The CD "White Light"

Sound [pure vibration], is the force inherent in all things, it has a powerful effect on the cellular structure of human beings and a very profound effect on our psyche and soul. In esoteric numerology each person's master number corresponds with a specific colour. Also associated with each colour is a musical composition. The White Light CD contains these 8 specific musical masterpieces, beautifully recorded, that when heard, will help bring into balance anyone whose master number corresponds to that particular colour.

Individual Essence Pyramid Packs

Stock essences for each of the individual White Light Essences are available. They come in the individual pyramid packs carefully developed to embrace and protect the beauty and potency of these wonderful essences.

Australian Bush Flower Essences Product Range

Australian Bush Flower Essences have a range of individual essences and a complete retail combination range including:

- 14 Combination Essences
- 5 Essence Mists • 5 Essence Creams

Ian has 3 other publications:

- Australian Bush Flower Essences
- Bush Flower Healing
- Australian Bush Flower Remedies (Reference Book)
- as well as Flower Insight Card packs.

individual essence drops

A range of 65 essences that can be used individually or combined to treat any specific application. These are available in stock concentrate or ready to use dose. A reference chart is available from Australian Bush Flower Essences to use as a selection guide.

A range of 14 essences formulated for specific application to assist with the whole family's emotional care and wellbeing. The unique dropper bottle makes application easy – simply take 7 drops under the tongue or in a glass of water morning and night.

Contact us for a free information pack on these essences and services including a complete workshop schedule. Also, if you would like to become a member of the Australian Bush Flower Essence Society (as a member you will recieve regular newsletter updates on all Australian Bush Flower Essences activities including White Light Essences, case histories, workshops, updates from around the world) please contact Bush Biotherapies Pty Ltd on
Phone: 02 9450 1388, International phone: 61 2 9450 1388
Fax: 02 9450 2866, Email: info@ausflowers.com.au,
or visit our website: www.ausflowers.com.au
or by posting to: 45 Booralie Road, Terrey Hills NSW 2084, Australia.

insight flower cards

essence mists

Specially formulated pure botanical essences are combined in a gentle mist to refresh, renew and revitalise the emotions, body, mind and psyche. These 5 unique blends are formulated for use at home, at work or with friends and loved ones.

essence creams

Exquisite blends of pure botanical essence creams formulated for emotional care and wellbeing are available in 5 combinations for everyday use. These deeply moisturising and nurturing creams are ideal for dry, flaking and sensitive skin conditions and can be used on all skin types encouraging natural health and beauty. [the body's own healing response]

Ian White, a fifth generation Australian Herbalist and Naturopath, has been practising as a healer for over 20 years. He is also the founder of the Australian Bush Flower Essences and author of:

'AUSTRALIAN BUSH FLOWER ESSENCES'

'BUSH FLOWER HEALING'

'AUSTRALIAN BUSH FLOWER REMEDIES' (Reference book)

Ian regularly conducts workshops on the Australian Bush Flower Essences and White Light Essences in Australia, Asia, Europe, North and South America.